JE

See special instructions
on inside front cover.

JE

Place tab in slit
at back edge of gown,
then fold tab over.
For going-away dress,
fold tab over right hand.

JE

Place tab in
slit at hand.

Wedding Gown

Plate 1

JE

JE

Yachting Dress

Going-away Dress

Plate 2

Place tab
behind head.

Place tab
behind head.

JE

JE

JE

Promenade Dress

Visiting Dress

Plate 3

Cut along
broken line at
back of head.

Plate 4

JE

JE

Negligee

Morning Dress

Riding Habit

Bathing Costume

Plate 5

Place tab in slit
at right hand.

JE

JA

Ballgown

Ballgown

Plate 6-Engagement Dinner and Ball

Place tab in slit at hands; fold tab over.

JA

JA

JA

At-home Dress

Bridesmaid's Dress

Plate 7

Afternoon Dress

Promenade Dress

JA

JA

Plate 8